HOW? WHO? WHAT? WHEN? WHERE? WHY?

Questions Kids ask

ABOUT
FOOD

PUBLISHER	Joseph R. DeVarennes
PUBLICATION DIRECTOR	Kenneth H. Pearson
ADVISORS	Roger Aubin
	Robert Furlonger
EDITORIAL SUPERVISOR	Jocelyn Smyth
PRODUCTION MANAGER	Ernest Homewood
PRODUCTION ASSISTANTS	Martine Gingras Kathy Kishimoto
	Catherine Gordon Peter Thomlison
CONTRIBUTORS	Alison Dickie Nancy Prasad
	Bill Ivy Lois Rock
	Jacqueline Kendel Merebeth Switzer
	Anne Langdon Dave Taylor
	Sheila Macdonald Alison Tharen
	Susan Marshall Donna Thomson
	Pamela Martin Pam Young
	Colin McCance
SENIOR EDITOR	Robin Rivers
EDITORS	Brian Cross Ann Martin
	Anne Louise Mahoney Mayta Tannenbaum
PUBLICATION ADMINISTRATOR	Anna Good
ART AND DESIGN	Richard Comely Ronald Migliore
	George Elliott Sue Wilkinson
	Greg Elliott

Canadian Cataloguing in Publication Data

Main entry under title:

Questions kids ask about food

(Questions kids ask ; 12)
ISBN 0-7172-2551-8

1. Food—Miscellanea—Juvenile literature.
2. Children's questions and answers.
I. Smyth, Jocelyn.   II. Comely, Richard.   III. Series.

TX355.Q47 1988   j641.3   C89-093083-X

Questions Kids Ask . . . about FOOD

continued

What type of food would you take on a trip into space?

Bet you never had to chase a flying meatball for dinner! You might if you were an astronaut. There's no weight, or gravity, in space. So everything floats around unless held on to or strapped down.

The first astronauts solved the problem of flyaway food by squeezing their meals out of tubes. But the food looked like baby food, and tasted even worse.

Now space food tastes the same as food on earth—it's just prepared differently. Space cookies are bite size, to fit in your mouth all at once. You don't want crumbs floating around and getting into the machinery! Other foods, such as macaroni and cheese, and scrambled eggs, are freeze-dried and vacuum-packed in individual cartons or pouches. Before you eat, you just add water from a dispenser that squirts in exactly the right amount. Liquid salt is also squeezed in and mixed.

Most of the food is made sticky enough to stay on a spoon so it won't float away as you try to eat it. Once a sandwich is made, it can't be put down or it will float apart!

DID YOU KNOW . . . scientists say insects would make an ideal food for space travel.

How did hamburgers get their name?

All it took was a simple request from a sailor away from home to start one of the biggest food trends ever.

The name probably got started in the early 1900s when German sailors arrived in New York and asked the short-order cooks there to prepare their meat the way they were used to eating it at home in Hamburg, Germany.

These ground meat patties served in a bun were an instant success at the St. Louis Fair in 1903. Since then, billions and billions of hamburgers have been eaten by young and old alike all over the world.

DID YOU KNOW . . . hot dogs also originated in Germany and were first known as frankfurters, franks, wieners, red hots and dachshund sausages.

Hurray!

Who invented pizza?

We don't know the name of the person who made the first pizza, but we do know that it was made in the city of Naples, Italy. Probably it was just the inspired idea of someone who had a family to feed and only bread and a few odds and ends to feed them with.

Although nowadays we put all sorts of toppings on pizzas—from shrimp to pineapple—the original pizza used only flat baked dough, anchovies, olive oil, tomatoes and cheese.

How did the sandwich get its name?

The sandwich was introduced in the eighteenth century by the English nobleman John Montagu, the fourth earl of Sandwich. It is said that the earl was so crazy about card games that he often played for as long as 24 hours without leaving the card table, even for meals. Instead, he ordered his servants to bring slices of cold beef between pieces of bread to the table so he could eat without interrupting his game. This way of eating became popular, and the sandwich was named in his honor.

What is the world's best-selling candy?

The world's best-selling candy is the candy with the hole in the middle—Life Savers. Between 1913 and 1987, 33 431 236 300 rolls were sold. One reason for their popularity may be that Life Savers come in such a wide variety of flavors. There's a flavor to suit every taste. Or maybe the name has something to do with it!

If you placed all the rolls of Life Savers sold between 1913 and 1987 end to end, the tunnel formed by the holes in the middle would stretch to the moon and back three times!

Who invented licorice?

You probably know licorice as a chewy candy that comes in black and red strips. Did you know that there's a licorice plant too?

It grows in southern Europe and Asia and has been used for thousands of years to flavor foods and as a medicine. The roots are about 1.2 metres (4 feet) long and are a bright yellow color. They are very sweet.

Millions of pounds of dried licorice root are brought into Canada and the United States every year. It is put in medicines to make them taste better and used to flavor soft drinks, candy, gum and many other things.

How is cotton candy made?

Cotton candy is the light fluffy cloud of candy that comes in pretty colors, usually pink and blue. It seems to be everywhere at fairs. Another name for it is candy floss.

It's made from sugar crystals spun in a large heated machine called a centrifuge. This produces light wads of fluff around the sides of the machine. These bits of fluff are collected by lightly touching them with a paper stick. Gradually the candy builds up so that soon it looks as if the stick is wearing a big, colorful candy wig. What looks like a huge amount to eat melts in your mouth in no time.

Why do onions make you cry?

Do you notice that as soon as you cut an onion your eyes begin to sting and water? This is because cutting releases an oil that contains sulfur and that very quickly forms a vapor. When the vapor reaches your eyes, it irritates them and makes them sting. Fortunately, there are nerves in your nose that are connected to your tear ducts. As soon as these nerves detect the vapor, they signal your tear ducts to start the tears streaming out, easing the sting.

One way to avoid tears is to cut onions under running water. This way the vapor is swept downward by the motion of the water.

DID YOU KNOW . . . onions are not native to North America. They originally came from Mongolia.

BOY! PEELING ONIONS SURE MAKES **YOU** CRY!

IT'S NOT THE ONIONS! YOU'RE STANDING ON MY **FOOT**!

Who were the first people to mash potatoes?

Centuries ago, an Inca dug up a potato and an important chapter in human history began.

The Incas harvested and ate potatoes in the Andes Mountains in South America. Potatoes grew well in the cool, moist climate and were a staple in the native diet. Their way of making potato flour sounds pretty funny, but it worked. They mashed the potatoes by walking on them! Then they set the broken pieces in the sun until they were dry enough to be ground into flour.

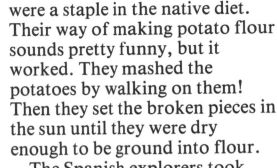

The Spanish explorers took potatoes back home with them and soon all European countries were growing potatoes. Today potatoes are an important food in many countries, including the Soviet Union, China, Poland and the United States.

Where do truffles come from?

Truffles are a strange food and they're gathered in an even stranger way. They look like lumpy mushrooms. You'll never see one growing because they grow underground, usually on or near the roots of oak trees, 8 to 30 centimetres (3 to 12 inches) down.

How, you might wonder, do people pick them if they can't see them? What you do is grab a pig, tie a leash on it, and go for a walk! Why? Because pigs can sniff the truffles' odor even through the ground.

If the pig seems to think there are truffles underground, you get out a shovel and start digging, so that you get there first—pigs love truffles. This is why trained dogs are often used instead. They can sniff the truffles out for you but won't gobble them up.

Where and why would you be served cooked insects?

What's for dinner? Beetle burgers and cockroach casserole. You may turn up your nose in disgust, but insects are a popular food for many people, especially in African countries, China and Japan.

Just about any insect you can think of—ants, termites, butterflies, grasshoppers—are eaten and enjoyed somewhere in the world. One reason is that insects are nutritious. They are a good source of protein and minerals. Some say they're delicious too. Termites taste like pineapple. Baked bees are dry and flaky and taste like a nutty breakfast cereal.

You may think that insects aren't clean, but they are no dirtier than any other animal people eat. When properly washed, insect meat is just as clean as beef, pork or chicken. Insects grow quickly, produce high-quality meat and are inexpensive to raise. They may be the food of the future.

Pass the chocolate-covered grasshoppers and candied wasp eggs, please. Mmm—delicious!

What types of food are served at a luau?

If you go to a Hawaiian luau (loo-ow), be prepared to *pig out*. A luau in the Hawaiian Islands always includes a whole young pig roasted in an underground oven called an *imu*. You'll also eat *poi* (po-ee) which is made from taro root. You scoop it out of a bowl and eat it with your fingers—like all the other food at the luau. There's steamed fish too, wrapped up in leaves. To end this huge meal, help yourself to bananas, guavas, pineapples and many other delicious fruits.

Luaus are as famous for their dancing and singing as they are for their food. Hula dancers dressed in skirts of leaves sway their hips and move their arms to music. The dancers' movements tell stories about the islands.

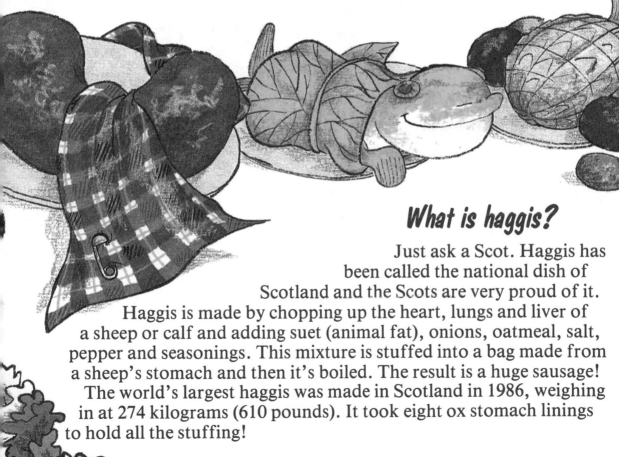

What is haggis?

Just ask a Scot. Haggis has been called the national dish of Scotland and the Scots are very proud of it. Haggis is made by chopping up the heart, lungs and liver of a sheep or calf and adding suet (animal fat), onions, oatmeal, salt, pepper and seasonings. This mixture is stuffed into a bag made from a sheep's stomach and then it's boiled. The result is a huge sausage!

The world's largest haggis was made in Scotland in 1986, weighing in at 274 kilograms (610 pounds). It took eight ox stomach linings to hold all the stuffing!

Who invented ice cream cones?

Ice cream cones were invented when someone rolled up a waffle and put ice cream in it so that people could walk around holding the waffle and licking the ice cream. The first time anybody did this was in 1904, at the World's Fair held in St. Louis, Missouri, in the United States. But who was the first person to do it?

There are two different stories. Mr. Abe Doumar, who ran a food stand at the fair, claimed that he thought of using a waffle to hold ice cream when they ran out of dishes at the ice cream stand beside him. The other story involves Mr. Charles E. Menches, who ran an ice cream stand at the fair. Charles was courting a woman who was on the other side of the fairgrounds, and he used to take her flowers and an ice cream sandwich. The sandwich was ice cream spread between two waffles. One time he took these presents to his girlfriend, but she didn't have a vase for the flowers, so she took one waffle and rolled it into a cone to carry the flowers in. Then she rolled up the ice cream in the other waffle, and presto! that was the first ice cream cone.

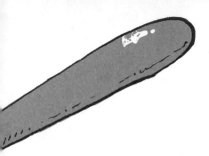

Why does milk turn sour?

If you've ever forgotten to put the milk back in the refrigerator and left it out overnight, you know that it can taste sour in the morning.

Milk doesn't take very long to turn sour if it isn't kept cold. That's because warm air is full of microbes—little living plant cells —like yeast mold. Microbes are so tiny that you need a microscope to see them. Like all plants, microbes need a substance to grow in. The substance they like best is a liquid with sugar or starch in it—like milk. When they're growing, these tiny plants change the sugar in milk to acids. And these acids make the liquid taste sour.

Microbes find it much harder to live in a cool liquid. Milk will stay sweet and fresh for days if you keep it cool in a refrigerator. But if you let the milk stand in a warm place, millions of microbes will move right in and begin to grow.

When were milkshakes invented?

Towards the end of the 1800s, ice cream parlors and soda fountains became popular. That's where people went to meet friends, and where couples went to talk and get to know each other better. One reason these places became so popular was that going out for ice cream treats was a new idea. Before that, most ice cream had been made at home. In 1851 a milk dealer named Jacob Fussell realized he could produce ice cream in large quantities for sale, and he did, starting a new trend.

Sodas, sundaes and milkshakes were all developed at this time, as the ice cream parlor owners experimented with various combinations of ice cream, jams, jellies, fruits, nuts and syrups.

Are all bananas yellow?

If you had a craving for a banana, would you choose a green one or a yellow one? Probably a yellow one. You know that green bananas are generally not yet ripe and their fruit will be hard and bitter. Bananas are picked when they are green so that by the time they arrive at the end of their long journey to North America, they are not over-ripe.

Some bananas are not normally eaten raw. These are a large kind of banana called a plantain. Their fruit is hard and starchy, so it is usually cooked before it's eaten. Have you ever eaten a greenish-yellow plantain?

Some ripe bananas are not yellow at all. The red Jamaica banana is—you guessed it!—red. It's a small banana that is not often seen in North America. The reason? The red Jamaica has a thin skin and as a result cannot be easily shipped. In Jamaica, bananas come in three colors: yellow, green and red.

What makes jelly jell?

Look at a recipe for making jelly and you'll see that the ingredients are very simple: fruit, sugar and water. Sometimes a few spices are added. So what makes jelly jell?

It's something in the fruit itself called pectin, which is a carbohydrate. When fruit or fruit juices are cooked with sugar, the pectin in the fruit makes the jelly thicken, or "jell."

The amount of pectin varies from fruit to fruit. And under-ripe fruit has more pectin than ripe fruit. Crab apples, cranberries, plums and red and black currants contain a lot of pectin.

Some jelly recipes combine fruits low in pectin with high-pectin fruits to make sure the jelly will jell. However, if you make mint jelly, you will have to add commercial liquid pectin, because mint leaves don't contain any natural pectin at all.

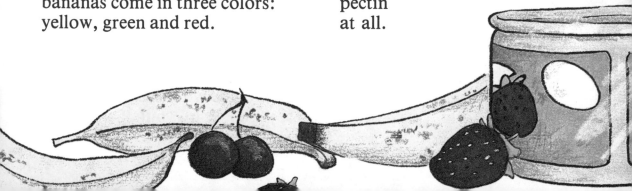

DID YOU KNOW . . . that a peanut is not a nut but a pea? So a peanut butter sandwich is actually a pea butter sandwich!

DID YOU KNOW . . . eating a spoonful of peanut butter is a good cure for the hiccups!

Why does peanut butter stick to the roof of your mouth?

How do you like your peanut butter—creamy or crunchy? Whatever type you prefer, most people love peanut butter. What you may not like is the way it sticks to the roof of your mouth.

Peanut butter has a "sticky-mouth feel" because of the hydration of the peanut protein. In other words, the high protein level of peanut butter draws moisture away from your mouth when you eat it. Result: the roof of your mouth gets very dry and the peanut butter sticks to it.

That's probably why people add moist things such as mashed banana, jelly or honey to their peanut butter sandwiches. It goes down easier and your mouth doesn't feel so dry. Some people are so afraid of peanut butter sticking to the roof of their mouth that there is even a name for their fear: arachibutyrophobia.

Do pickles grow on trees?

When Peter Piper picked a peck of pickled peppers, he couldn't possibly have picked them from a tree. Pickles don't grow on trees. In fact, pickles don't *grow* anywhere. A pickle is any food that has been preserved in vinegar and salt.

Most people immediately think of a pickled cucumber when they hear the word "pickle." This is because cucumbers are the most common vegetable pickled. But any kind of food can be pickled, and meats, fruits and other kinds of vegetables are often pickled too. You may have tasted pickled pigs' feet, pickled pears, pickled peaches—or perhaps Peter's famous pickled peppers.

In making pickles, the fruit, vegetable or meat is usually first soaked in brine (heavily salted water) and vinegar. Then it's flavored with seasonings such as mustard, dill, horseradish, cinnamon, allspice, cloves, celery seed, peppercorns and pimento. Sometimes sugar is added too. Once everything has been well mixed together, the mixture is sealed tightly in jars and usually stored in a cool place until it's ready to be eaten.

DID YOU KNOW . . . about $500 million worth of pickle products are made each year. Peter Piper could be busy picking pecks of pickles for a long time.

18

Why do people in hot countries eat spicy food?

Mexican and South American food contains a lot of hot chili peppers. East Indians eat hot curries. Why do people in hot countries eat such hot foods? One reason is to cool off!

Sounds strange, but it's true. Hot, spicy food makes you sweat, and as the sweat evaporates, it cools you off. You can test this for yourself by eating something hot and spicy this summer.

There's another reason for making food hot and spicy. Before people had refrigerators, food spoiled quickly, especially in hot climates. The hot spices helped to slow down the spoiling process.

Where does table salt come from?

To say that someone is the salt of the earth is a common way to describe a person who is very dependable. This old saying also tells us something about where salt comes from.

Salt is a mineral found in many of the rocks that make up the earth's crust. (Sea water also has salt in it, but most of the salt we use comes from deep in the ground.) It comes from layers of rock salt that were created when salty seas of long ago dried up. Through the years the salt was covered with other rocks.

It's not difficult to get table salt from the layers of rock salt underground. Mines are dug deep down into the earth and the salt is taken out in blocks. Or water is piped to the salt and then pumped up again. The salt that has been dissolved in the water can easily be taken back out of it.

DID YOU KNOW . . . the "Uncle Ben" of Uncle Ben's Rice was a Persian who invented a way of canning cooked rice for soldiers' rations during World War II.

What plant feeds half the world's population?

"Have you had your rice today?"

If you were in China that would be your greeting as you met old friends. It is their way of saying "How do you do," and with good reason. If you hadn't had your rice today in China, you wouldn't be doing very well at all!

Nearly half the world's population relies partly or almost entirely on rice for food, and that includes the Chinese. People in Asian countries eat between 90 and 225 kilograms (200 to 500 pounds) of rice a year. Even in North America it is a popular food, although only about 4 kilograms (8 pounds) are eaten by each person in a year.

Rice is the grain of the rice plant, a type of grass. Each plant has several stems, and between 50 and 150 grains of rice grow on each stem. That would only be enough rice for a few mouthfuls, but if you add up all the rice grown in the world, it is enough to feed billions of people. Over 180 thousand million kilograms (400 thousand million pounds) are grown and eaten annually.

What is sushi?

Would you ever consider eating a piece of raw fish? To some people this idea sounds very strange. But in Japan, raw fish is enjoyed by everyone. In fact, a very popular food is a dish called sushi.

Sushi are tiny balls of cold rice that have been soaked in vinegar. The rice is wrapped in *nori* (seaweed) and a piece of raw fish or seafood is placed on top of each one. Then they are carefully arranged and served on beautiful trays.

The Japanese have never been big meat eaters, but they have been eating raw fish for a long time. A legend says that hundreds of years ago an emperor was served raw clams. He liked them so much he made the cook his head chef. From then on, it became popular in Japan to eat raw fish.

Does all corn pop?

Not all corn pops. The type that does is specially grown to be used as popcorn.

Each popcorn kernel has a hard, tough coating which is waterproof. When a kernel is heated, this covering stops the natural moisture inside from escaping. If the kernel is heated enough, the moisture turns to steam and makes the kernel explode. Pop! The result is delicious—soft, puffy popcorn.

Why does soda pop have bubbles?

In some parts of the world there are pockets of water below the earth's surface containing very high levels of minerals. Not only is this water good for you, but it also has bubbles, just like pop.

In 1772 an Englishman named Joseph Priestly decided to manufacture imitation mineral water. He put soda in plain water to make it fizzy.

The method used today is to add carbon dioxide gas to the water. The bubbling is the result of the gas trying to escape. When there's a lot

Why does a doughnut have a hole?

Doughnuts have been made for hundreds of years by frying dough in deep fat, but the hole is a recent invention. In 1847, as the legend goes, a Dutch-American sea captain called Hanson Gregory cut holes in the center of his doughnuts because he thought it would make them more digestible. Why he thought this no one knows; however, everyone seemed to like the new shape. So much so, in fact, that a plaque was put up to mark Hanson Gregory's birthplace in Rockport, Maine.

Doughnuts are now so popular that many restaurants even sell the "holes."

of gas in a bottle or can, you'll hear a loud sound when you open it. That's where the name *pop* comes from.

Most pop is made by combining carbonated water, flavoring and sugar.

Who made the first chocolate bars?

Do you think about soldiers when you unwrap a chocolate bar? Well, if you did, it wouldn't be as strange as it might seem.

In 1876 solid milk chocolate was invented in Switzerland. Up until then, most people had enjoyed chocolate only as a drink—just as we drink hot chocolate today.

The popularity of solid chocolate was slow to spread, however—that is, until World War I. Then, because chocolate is a quick-energy food and easy to carry around (and easy to eat!), thousands upon thousands of chocolate bars were made for soldiers to eat to keep up their strength. Because everyone loves chocolate, the soldiers sometimes used their chocolate bars to bargain with, to get themselves out of a tight spot.

Where does chocolate come from? It's made from the beans of the cacao evergreen tree. The beans are cleaned, roasted, hulled and then ground. Then they are mixed with whole milk solids and granulated sugar to make solid milk chocolate.

DID YOU KNOW . . . for centuries the Aztecs used cacao beans as money. Did Aztec parents tell their children not to put money in their mouths the way yours probably do?

What are curds and whey?

Little Miss Muffet
Sat on her tuffet
Eating her curds and whey

You probably remember this as part of a Mother Goose rhyme. But did you ever wonder what it was Miss Muffet was eating?

To understand what curds and whey are, you need to know something about how cheese is made.

First the milk is pasteurized. It is then placed in large tanks to be heated a second time. A "starter culture" composed of bacteria is poured in, causing the milk to curdle or sour. Next, a substance made from enzymes found in the stomachs of calves is added. The milk now has the consistency of wet lumpy custard.

The solid parts are known as curds, the liquid as whey. After the whey is drained off, the curds are pressed together and allowed to age until they become cheese.

Little Miss Muffet was eating her cheese before it was ready.

How is butter made?

To make butter all you have to do is get a small carton of heavy cream (35%) and shake it. The motion will cause butterfat, contained in the cream, to separate and float to the surface. You've just made butter! Be warned, however, you may have to shake it for a long time.

Large dairy companies make butter in almost the same manner but on a much larger scale. First they pasteurize the cream by

24

heating it to a temperature of 85°C (185°F) for 15 seconds. This kills any harmful bacteria that might cause the butter to go bad.

After the cream has stood for several hours it is poured into a large machine that churns—beats and shakes—it. As the cream is raised and revolved, bubbles start to form and butterfat collects around them in layers. These pea-sized lumps, called granules, float to the surface. When the air bubbles inside them collapse, the churning is completed and the remaining liquid drained off.

The butter is next rinsed in cold water and salt is sometimes added to flavor and help preserve it.

The only thing left for the company to do is cut and package the butter in the convenient sizes we buy in the supermarket.

What makes the holes in Swiss cheese?

A slice of Swiss cheese isn't just tasty; it's full of holes too. Did you think perhaps a little mouse had a few early nibbles? No—the holes in Swiss cheese are made by bacteria.

When cheese makers are making Swiss cheese, they add a bacteria called *propionibacteria*. They mix the ingredients and then put the cheese in storage to develop. This is called curing. While the cheese is curing, the bacteria give off carbon dioxide gas which makes gas bubbles in the cheese. When the cheese is sliced, the bubbles become holes.

THIS ONE JUST DOESN'T HAVE ENOUGH **HOLES** TO LOOK SWISS!

You wouldn't want a hole in your pocket or in your shoe, but you do want holes in Swiss cheese. Without the holes, Swiss cheese just wouldn't be the same.

What is a baked Alaska?

You don't have to bake Alaska (a land of ice and snow) to make this yummy dessert. The name refers to the combination of something hot—baked meringue—with something cold—ice cream.

You start with a brick of ice cream that is frozen very hard. Place it in the center of a sponge cake and cover the cake with meringue. Bake the cake in the oven for only five minutes at a very high temperature. This is the tricky part. You have to time it just right—you want the meringue to turn golden brown, but you don't want the ice cream to melt. Then eat it right away.

Where does sugar come from?

Did you know that until the great voyages of discovery honey was the only sweetener that people in Europe ever used? Sugar was unknown in Europe until only a few centuries ago. When it first appeared, it was used as a medicine and was very expensive.

Today, sugar comes from two main sources: sugar beets and sugar cane. Sugar beets are large white beets. Sugar cane is a tall reed that grows in thick clumps, taller than a person. To get sugar, both beets and cane are crushed and pressed. Heavy sweet liquid is forced out, which is then refined to make sugar, or sucrose.

There are other kinds of sugar as well. Fruits contain their own kind of sugar—fructose. Notice next time you drink milk that it tastes sweet—that's from milk sugar, or lactose.

DID YOU KNOW . . . the province of Quebec produces most of the maple products in North America.

How is maple syrup made?

Maple syrup and maple sugar come from the sap of sugar maple, red maple and black maple trees. What is sap? It's the juice inside the tree that helps it grow—something like our blood.

Sap is taken from the trees in late winter and early spring. There are two ways of doing this. The old-fashioned way is very easy but takes a long time. Holes are drilled in the trunk of the tree so that a hollow spout can be inserted. The sap drips out of the spout into a bucket that's been hung just below.

The new way skips the bucket stage. All the spouts are connected to a pipe that takes the sap straight to where it is turned into syrup and maple sugar.

No matter how the sap is collected, the next step is to boil it down in a shallow pan to develop the flavor and golden color. It takes 132-170 litres (35-45 gallons) of sap to make 3.8 litres (1 gallon) of syrup. If the syrup is boiled down even further, it becomes hard maple sugar.

What is junk food?

Junk is what people throw away because they don't need it. Foods such as potato chips, doughnuts, candy and soda pop are called junk foods because your body doesn't need them. They won't keep you healthy or help you grow (except fatter) because they're low in nutrients, or food value.

There's no denying that most junk food tastes great—and almost everybody does eat some. Small amounts aren't harmful, but if you eat too much of it, you may have no room left for the foods your body does need. So next time you crave potato chips, try biting into an apple instead!

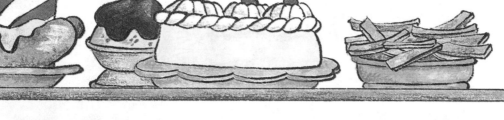

How much food do you eat in a year?

Imagine 20 shopping carts filled with food. That's the amount the average North American will consume in one year. And it weighs about a tonne.

So what's in those shopping carts? 67 kilograms (147 pounds) of bread, rice and cereals; 105 kilograms (231 pounds) of meat, poultry, fish, eggs, beans and nuts; 100 kilograms (220 pounds) of milk products; 287 kilograms (632 pounds) of fruit and vegetables, including 70 kilograms (154 pounds) of potatoes; and 311 kilograms (685 pounds) of other food, including 40 kilograms (88 pounds) of sugar.

However, North Americans buy and serve more food than they need—and a lot of it ends up in the garbage. We throw out about 10 garbage cans full of wasted food per person every year. That's a quarter of the food you started with in all those shopping carts!

Why are food additives put in food?

Chemical additives are put in food for many reasons. They keep food tasting and looking fresh. They make ice cream stay creamy and crackers crisp; they keep fats and oils from turning sour. And they also add color and flavor.

Here are some additives and what they do. Fructose and glucose are kinds of sugar used for flavor and sweetness. Cornstarch makes food firm (as in marshmallows). Gelatin makes food fluffy and tender. Glycerine (added to chewing gum) gives texture and body and helps retain moisture. Lecithin helps food stay mixed and not separate out. Beta-carotene gives an orange-yellow color. Sodium nitrate is added to wieners and bacon to give the meat a reddish color.

Most milk, bread and cereals have vitamins added to replace the natural vitamins lost in the manufacturing process. Minerals are often added to bread and cereals along with the vitamins.

DID YOU KNOW . . .
caffeine, which is a stimulant, is added to some soft drinks and to chocolate.

Is it safe to eat a thousand-year-old egg?

Yes. You may have never tasted one, but Chinese people consider what they call a ''thousand-year-old egg'' a great delicacy. The name, however, is quite an exaggeration since the eggs are really months, not years, old.

What's the secret recipe? The Chinese cover duck eggs in a mixture of ashes, tea, lime and salt to preserve them. Then they roll the eggs in dry rice husks and bury them in the ground. Some months later, when they think the eggs are ready, they dig them up. The hard outer covering is broken off, and the eggs are shelled—just like hard-boiled eggs.

What happens to the eggs while they are in the ground? The yolks turn an orange-green color; the whites solidify into something that looks like dark green jelly. Now they are ready to eat. They are served as appetizers on toothpicks with thin slices of fresh ginger.

Can you make soup out of a bird's nest?

Have you ever thought of making soup out of a bird's nest? Amazingly enough, it can be done. In fact, bird's nest soup is a great delicacy in China.

Of course, you can't use just any old bird's nest for soup. You need the nests of cave swiftlets, tiny birds of the swift family that build their nests entirely from their own saliva.

Chinese nest collectors gather the milky colored, saucer-shaped nests and sell them to markets and restaurants, which pay very high prices for this little bird's home!

What is the world's largest dish?

A stuffed turkey at Christmas seems pretty big. So does a pig or lamb roasted on a spit at a special outdoor barbecue. Friends, family and relatives all help themselves, and there's still lots of food left over.

But these dishes look small beside the largest dish in the world. And to make it, you need a camel! First stuff cooked eggs into some fish. Then stuff the fish into cooked chickens. Stuff the chickens into a roasted sheep. Finally stuff the sheep into a whole camel and roast it.

This dish is occasionally prepared by the Bedouin (a desert tribe in Arabia) for their wedding feasts. However, you'll have to imagine what it tastes like— unless you're lucky enough to get invited to a Bedouin wedding.

Do you mind! I still need this.

Index _____